Blighty Brighton

photographs & memories of Brighton in the First World War

QueenSpark Books
& the Lewis Cohen Urban Studies Centre
at Brighton Polytechnic

HELP
"THE SECOND LINE OF DEFENCE."

BYAM·SHAW del 1917

SATURDAY, JULY 14t.

WOMEN'S DAY

With the support of the MAYORS OF BRIGHTON and HOVE and
the co-operation of all the Women's Organisations in the Boroughs,

FOR PROVIDING

HUTS FOR WOMEN MUNITION WORKERS & THE AUXILIARY ARMY IN FRANC

contents

Take me back to dear old Bligh-ty, Bligh-ty is the place for me

When this bloo-dy war is o-ver, Oh how hap-py I will be

Blighty

"Take me back to dear old Blighty

Blighty is the place for me ...."

Blighty - England, home, away from the trenches where one felt safe and could get hot food, a warm bed and feminine company. A nostalgic memory of happy times before the war or a hope for the future.

"When this bloody war is over

Oh how happy I will be."

The word could be used as an adjective, Blighty butter was good fresh butter. A Blighty bag was used at casualty clearing stations to carry the wounded man's personal belongings when he knew he was homeward bound. Above all "a Blighty one" which was a wound, not too disabling but sufficiently serious to get a man away from the trenches and back to England; something most infantrymen longed for.

For many men suffering on the Western Front, a day trip or a holiday to Brighton before the war must have been their "Blighty". A memory of relaxed happy times with no discomfort or fear of impending death. So we have called this book "Blighty Brighton".

Like many words in British army slang "Blighty" originated in India; either it is a corruption from the Hindustani word "Biliak" for foreign country or England, or it comes from Urdu, "Becait" means strange or foreign, and through "Becanti" finally became "Blighty".

ARRIVAL OF OUR WOUNDED SOLDIERS FROM THE FRONT ENTERING NEW GRAMMAR SCHOOL BRIGHTON (SEPT. 1. 1914) F.A. WILES BRIGHTON

Introduction

The two World Wars were very different in many respects. Two differences are particularly important in understanding the impact of the wars on the British people.

Firstly, the expectation of what war would be like and how it would affect the individual varied greatly at the start of the two conflicts. In September 1939 there was anxiety and fear, mingled with resignation, because the war had been forced on Britain. The Second World War began only twenty years after the end of the Great War, the war to end all wars. The horror of trench warfare was still a living memory and people expected this to be repeated on a larger scale. Moreover throughout the 1930s, people had seen newsreel images of death raining down from the skies on civilian populations in China, Abyssinia and Spain. Expert and public opinion expected massive civilian casualties from aerial bombardments using gas as well as high explosives. Appeasement, attempts to keep the peace by giving way to the dictators, had great public support. When war was forced on the British in 1939 there were few illusions about the glories of war.

In August 1914 the atmosphere was different. There was great opposition to Britain's entry in to a European conflict and some prophets realised how devastating the war would become, but there was also great patriotic enthusiasm for what was seen as a noble and exciting adventure. Lord Grey, Foreign Secretary at the time that the war started, made one of the most famous statements in British history: "The lights are going out all over Europe, we shall not see them lit again in our lifetime." About the same time, in the House of Commons, he also said: "If we are engaged in war, we shall suffer but little more than we shall suffer if we stand aside."

Most of British public opinion seemed to agree with him. The general expectation was that it would be a short war, over by Christmas, fought by a professional army and

From East to West for the Motherland.

causing little interference in civilian life. Men rushed to volunteer, fearing the war would be over before they could get in to it. When Lord Kitchener, Minister of War, predicted that the war would last three years and need three million men to fight it he was largely ignored.

Why this enthusiastic rush to war? The last great European war the British had been engaged in was 100 years in the past. During the nineteenth century, wars for the British had been 'away matches' fought by small professional armies, isolated from civil society, in distant lands. They had been enjoyed as 'spectator sports' and even the Crimean and Boer wars were small in comparison with 20th Century conflicts. A great European war had been expected since the beginning of the 20th Century. Opposing alliances had formed, arms races and diplomatic crises all pointed the way. So the mobilisations and declarations of war in the summer of 1914 were no surprise, but the British expected to play only a small part in the land war.

Young Europeans, Britons among them, were eager and enthusiastic to serve their country, even to make 'The Final Sacrifice' if necessary. Death was romanticised by using Latin tags, 'Dulce et decorum est pro patria mori' (it is sweet and fitting to die for one's country). Old men told young men that they would be tested and not found wanting in battle, that war would improve the moral fibre of the nation. Some mothers really did say that they were ready to sacrifice their sons for their country, and young women gave white feathers, as a mark of cowardice to young men still in civilian clothing. So despite some misgivings there was a 'war fever' that swept over Europe in the summer of 1914, before reality set in.

The second difference that needs stressing is summed up in the titles given to the two wars; the 1914/18 war became 'The Great War', the conflict of 1939/45 war was known as 'The People's War'.

Civilians in the first war were bombed and bombarded from the sea but such attacks on civilian populations never reached the same intensity as the 'Blitz' on British cities in the Second World War. Another way of putting this is that there was a much sharper distinction between civilian and military experiences in the First War. The dominating symbol of the first war was the Western Front while in the second it was 'the Blitz' and 'Britain can take it'. Casualty figures bear this out, although in both wars military casualties were greater than civilian casualties, there was a much more even burden of sacrifice in the Second World War.

In the First World War, there were 1500 civilian deaths to 750,000 military; in the Second World War, 50,000 civilian deaths to 250,000 military. In the First World War there was no invasion threat yet the war was very close, just on the other side of the Channel. The sound of the guns could be heard on the south coast of England. Postal services in the trenches during quiet periods were regular and newspapers arrived on time. Men came back on leave from the horrors of the trenches to Victoria station in a matter of hours, still in mud-caked uniforms and with their rifles. But there was also a sharp distinction between the 'front line' and 'Blighty'; the relative safety of Britain and the very strict censorship maintained this isolation. Sometimes soldiers on leave felt this isolation as a sense of unreality. They used the refrain of a popular song: 'And when we tell them ... they'll never believe us', to explain how difficult it was to communicate to civilians the experience of trench warfare.

Second World War soldiers were much more civilians in uniform. The British army in the First War became a conscript army, but it reflected the hierarchy and rigid class system of Edwardian England. Officers were gentlemen, even if temporary gentlemen, other ranks were supposed to obey orders blindly and without question. In the First War British soldiers were shot for cowardice or desertion, in the Second War, none suffered this penalty for these crimes. In the First World War, shell-shock was grudgingly accepted in extreme cases; in the Second World War, it was recognised that every soldier had a breaking point and became subject to Battle Fatigue. There were more front line soldiers in the First War and the "Poor Bloody Infantry" suffered extreme conditions for longer periods, suffering heavier casualties and were less well cared for out of the front line than their equivalents in the Second World War.

Soldiers marching along Dyke Road from the 2nd Eastern General Hospital

KING'S ROAD, BRIGHTON.

Summer 1914

There were trams, and a few motor cars were beginning to appear, and only horses and carts to do the pulling of the tradesmen's wares. The roads had block surfaces where the tram lines ran, the rest were just dirt tracks, very muddy when it rained, and the dust blew up in clouds when it was dry. Children played in the roads and often had a long skipping rope across the road, it was great fun.

Men with hand barrows pushed their wares along, each season had its own special things for sale. March was the herring time, with shoals of fish off Brighton. Men with barrow loads of fish came through the street shouting "herrings 24 a shilling"; and the ladies came out of their houses to buy them. Fruits of each season came along in their order.

There was the organ grinder, with his little monkey dressed in a coat and holding a tin for us to put our pennies in, the jam jar and bottle man, with his windmills and balloons. Men and women singing in the streets, often selling lavender; big carts for carrying coal with strong cart horses.

The parks and gardens through the town were covered in by high iron railings, keepers closed the gates at sunset and rang a bell to warn people to get out.

Brighton seafront was clean, with no trader's shops or amusements. Black Rock was countrified with no houses beyond Kemp Town. We loved playing in the rock pools and were quite content with our buckets and spades when the tide was out. Small concert parties for people to enjoy took place in little buildings with a platform stage, and there were bathing machines for people to undress in, I remember using one.

opposite below: Egremont Street

North Street and Western Road had nice shops, where one could be served at counters and be talked to without hurry, the assistants took an interest in each customer.

King Edward died after only about seven years reign. I remember that at playtime in our school we girls had to wear black hair ribbons and had to walk quietly about the playground making no noise. Then if I remember, in 1911 King George V had his Coronation, all the schools in Brighton dressed in their school colours and marched to Preston Park to celebrate; the hot water for the tea was boiled in a steam engine, it tasted smoky. We had paper bags of buns and cakes and a china Coronation Mug to keep, I was pleased to take mine home and used it for tea.

So the time passed peacefully, there were sorrows among the people, children caught fevers and the "Fever Van" was always carrying them to the "Fever Hospital" on the hill. Sadly a great many children died and we used to stand quietly watching as the small white coffins were brought out. All funerals had hearses drawn by horses, usually black ones, with black plumes on their heads.

Hilda Barber

I was born, one of six children, on Albion Hill in 1898. My father had tuberculosis. I left Park Street School at 14. My future husband was taken to Preston Barracks at the age of sixteen by his father who took the shilling given to all new recruits. He had been in the army for two years when war broke out and he was sent to France with the Second Sussex Regiment, who were the first over the top. He was badly injured and sent home, with his arm was shattered; later a doctor said it should have been amputated as it had splintered. He never worked, he was an invalid for 63 years and only had a small pension to live on.

Alice Ethel Sharp

10

FOOD PANIC SUBSIDING

The panic over provisions is subsiding. Inquiries made yesterday among the business houses of the town revealed the satisfactory fact that people who temporarily lost their heads are regaining them, and that the raid on the provision stores is ceasing. The provision shops yesterday presented their normal appearance.

There is no getting away from the fact that the declaration of war produced a general panic in regard to our food supply. In a state of excitement, for which of course every allowance can be made, people besieged the grocers and provision merchants, as well as the bakers, and overwhelmed them with enormously increased orders. People who ordinarily order enough for a week were provisioning for a month, many laid in enough for a year. It is a fact that people who in the ordinary way would consume two pounds of bacon a week were buying whole sides and carrying it away themselves so as to make sure of getting it. Many instances have come to our knowledge of people who have purchased enough flour to last them for a year. What they are going to do with such large stores one can hardly imagine. The idea seems to be to make one's own bread.

Brighton & Hove Herald 8 August 1914

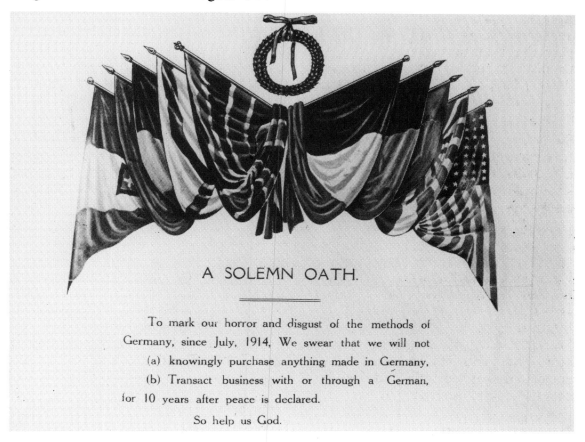

A SOLEMN OATH.

To mark our horror and disgust of the methods of Germany, since July, 1914, We swear that we will not

(a) knowingly purchase anything made in Germany,

(b) Transact business with or through a German,

for 10 years after peace is declared.

So help us God.

Fears about German economic competition, existing before the war, were the basis of anti-German propaganda during the war.

Allen West Ltd, a firm of electrical engineers founded in 1910, had a factory in Lewes Road. The firm's major development occured after the First World War and during the Second World War, when it produced thousands of radar sets and sections for Mulberry Harbours. In the First World War the firm produced a variety of war equipment, including hand grenades and the shells for the famous Stokes Mortar.

Notes taken from The Allen West Story April 1960

Allen West & Co Ltd was incorporated on April 15th 1910. After little more than four years of hard "pioneering" effort, plans has to be hastily reorganised - Britain was at war with Germany. During the 1914-18 hostilities, the works - with a nucleus of staff supplemented by largely untrained, average & "C3" men - were steadily engaged in making munitions, including the 106 Fuse, the Mills bomb, a spring-loaded bomb thrower (supplies of which were stored temporarily under the grandstand of Brighton racecourse), aeroplane parts, and the famous Stokes mortar shell. The Stokes mortar was officially adopted by the authorities after hurried trials on the battlefield in France. The Company in Brighton had actually designed the firing head and made the first 100 rounds of ammunition for the mortar in just 5 days. The trials at the Front were so successful that the Stokes Mortar gained official war Office recognition.

THE BOMB MYTH

One of the most widespread and at the same time one of the most mischievous of the many wild rumours that have been flying about is that bombs have been discovered at the houses of Germans or other aliens in Brighton.

This is a lie that should be nailed to the counter at once. We have the express authority of the Chief Constable for saying that no bombs or explosive material of any kind have been found in any house in Brighton.

The police have been deluged with communications about supposed spies, bombs, illicit wireless telegraph apparatus, and so on. They have investigated every complaint, and they are able to state positively that all are the product of excited imaginations.

A supposed spy has been arrested, as is shown elsewhere; and certain men whose movements were not readily explained have been put to rigorous inspection. The result is that nothing of an alarming character has been found. The public can be absolutely assured on the point. If you have suspicions of any one, tell the police by all means. But do not announce your suspicions to the world at large as facts.

...we are not at war with the individuals of the German colony in Brighton - harmless, respectable men and women finding themselves, by no fault of their own, at war with the country of their adoption, and torn with grief and anxiety knowing not what the morrow may bring forth. Do not let us libel them.

Brighton & Hove Herald 15 August 1914

opposite: portrait of an under-age volunteer on the Western Front in 1915, used in the campaign to introduce conscription, with the caption, "He did not wait to be asked".

LOCAL PRECAUTIONS AGAINST ALIENS

... All aliens have to report themselves at the police station and be registered. The obligation is also placed on all householders to give notice to the police of the presence of aliens in their houses. Such aliens must not travel more than five miles from their place of residence without permission, and must notify any change of address. Except with written permission, aliens must not have in their possession any firearms, ammunition, or explosives. They are prohibited from having more than three gallons of petrol or inflammable substance, from possessing signal apparatus, carrier or homing pigeons, or any motor car, motor cycle, or aircraft. Cipher or secret correspondence is also forbidden. The police have full authority to search any suspected place.

We learn that as many as 600 registrations are expected in Brighton. Aliens were freely registering at the police office yesterday. The German Club in Clarence-square is under strict police supervision, and special note has been taken of all who use it.

Brighton & Hove Herald 8 August 1914

Brighton in 1914 was London-by-the-Sea, a place for the city dweller to breathe the sea air on a day trip or for a longer stay. Further from town than Southend, but near enough and more sophisticated so it attracted a wider variety of holidaymakers.

At the turn of the century Brighton had been in decline, but after 1908, when Edward VII began to visit the town, it became once more a fashionable resort. Visitors and commuters were already using well established London, Brighton and South Coast Railway Services and at the turn of the century the petrol engine opened up the possibility of motoring down to Brighton. In 1905 the first motor omnibus service between London and Brighton was opened. The first aeroplane flew into Brighton in 1911, cinemas opened, theatres flourished. Day trippers flocked in and there was a "Sussex Fortnight" for high society.

But there was also another side to life in Edwardian Brighton. It was a large town, population 131,000 and just after West Ham it was the second most densely populated county borough in England. this meant that inside the ring of large Edwardian villas and close to the sea front there were dense urban slums. Brighton was more industrialised than other south coast resorts, many workers were underpaid and exploited in the service industries, but there were also areas of artisan workshops and small factories in the centre of the town. Several breweries, the gas works, Cox's Pill Factory and other concerns provided employment, but the largest industrial employer was the railway company. Large numbers serviced the communication system itself. There was also the Brighton Railway Works employing over 2000 people in repairing and building rolling stock and engines. This meant an established railway community with railway housing, an institute and a library.

Brighton in 1914 was not just a seaside town, it was a town of extremes of poverty and wealth.

Total War

On August the fourth the paper boys were shouting that Britain was at war with Germany! The Kaiser had invaded Belgium, recruiting was put into full swing, so the black cloud of war descended on our tranquil town of Brighton. We sang "God our help in ages past" for the opening hymn at school. Soon children were saying "my dad's gone to the war or my brothers are in the trenches in France". The young men were all eager to "join up" and some lads of sixteen put their ages up.

Khaki clad troops came marching through the town singing "Sussex by the Sea" and "Tipperary". One day Prince Edward of Wales visited Brighton, he went to Allen West and Patcham, people lined each side of Preston Road. I went down and saw him walking in front with the officers ahead and the troops behind, he looked very young; a cheer went up as he passed, it was quite a thrill to see royalty in the flesh. The weeks went by, men were simply being mown down and the trenches were in a terrible state, we were losing the cream of British manhood.

At Christmas a "cease-fire" took place over the two days and English and German men came out of the trenches and exchanged handshakes and cigarettes, then the two days were over and the killing began again. Those were sad and terrible days, mothers were losing their sons, children their fathers. Girls in my school would come crying to school because their father or brothers had been killed.

Food wasn't good, sugar was scarce and potatoes short, we ate swedes instead; flour was mixed with other things, called "standard flour". My father, who was a baker was

Our Wounded Soldiers in the Royal Sussex County Hospital '16.

very worried because he could not make good bread with it. There was hardly any butter, we had a sort of margarine called "nuts and milk" at 6d a pound from the Maypole in London Road, which we liked.

Soon wounded men were being sent home, schools were used for hospitals, Ditchling Road School was taken over and the children came to our school in Preston Road, so we only had half-day lessons either morning or afternoon.

The Dome and Pavilion became hospitals for wounded Indians, we used to go down and talked to them through the railings with nods and smiles, sometimes a whole Charabanc of them would be taken to the Duke of York's Cinema in Preston Circus. The Germans were using poisoned gas and a lot of men suffered damage to their lungs.

Time passed and the struggle went on, we only had partial black out, but when it was said that a German Zeppelin would come over, all windows were covered up. There were some bombs dropped on London I believe.

Women were busy in munitions factories and lots of helmets, gloves, socks and mittens were knitted to keep our troops warm. I knitted one sock, but I don't think any soldier would be very comfortable wearing it!

Hilda Barber

When the 1914 war came I started work as a tram conductor. After a year my friend, Nellie Penfold, and I decided to go to Willesden, London to work in a filling factory. I did not go into the DNT room which sent your skin yellow, because Nell had chilblains

16

and they would not part friends, so we worked on mercury. As I was pressing a detonator it went off and hit me in my right side and I had to go to the first aid post. We did not work when there was lightning, even sheet lightning.

We stayed in a hostel the first night in London and the next day they found us lodgings. We did night work 10.00 pm to 7.00 am, so decided to come home after the first year and started work at Allen West. I was on a machine on shell caps and had good money there.

Dolly Goldsmith (below)

My parents Fred Briggs and Florence Blundell became engaged in 1912, they married in 1913 and my brother was born in May 1914 and I followed in August 1916. My father was 20 and my mother about 17. Both my parents came from Brighton, my mother's family living at 40 William Street and my father's in Gloucester Terrace.

When I was born my father was already in the Army, but I doubt if he volunteered, he was probably called up during that year. He was a porter for a furniture dealers and enlisted in Hove. He was twenty three when I was born, but he was dead by the age of twenty five. I have a letter from the Commonwealth War Graves Commission about my father's death: "Private F. Briggs 69273, serving with 6th Battalion The Queens, died on 30th August 1918 and is buried in Plot 8, Row A, Grave 62 in a Communal Cemetery Extension, France. He formerly served with the Royal Sussex Regiment and is buried in a village in the depth of the Somme. My mother was very sensitive and she felt that something had happened to my father and she received a telegram later that day.

I was very young when my father died and I have only vague memories of him. I remember my father dressed in 'putties', which were like bandages on the bottom of the trousers to protect the legs from mud. He was kneeling down in front of our black chiffonier that had bright red glass doors, cleaning his buttons using a button stick to protect his uniform. This was probably during his last leave.

My mother had no help from anyone when he died, she had to go to work to support us. My grandmother (my father's mother) looked after us while my mother went out to work. She got a pension of 10/- a week for herself, 7/6 per week for my brother and 5/- per week for me. When we left school she lost her allowances. She must have already been working on the trams when my father died, because she started as a conductress and ended up as a driver, before losing her job when the men returned from the war.

My mother was a happy, outgoing sort of person, so I think she enjoyed the work on the trams. She worked from the Lewes Road Depot and she was on the Lewes Road route. My mother would sometimes talk in her sleep, she would sit up and say 'Lewes Road, do you want it or not?'

I can remember the Christmas party held at the tram depot in 1918. I was only 2 years 4 months but I can remember having a free ride on the tram to the depot and a very large Christmas tree.

My father's medals and a plate were on the wall until my mother re-married seven years later, then she took them down and gave them to my brother.

When my mother lost her job on the trams she had to find another job to help support us. She was a marvellous dancer and she took a job in a dance hall in Gloucester Place as a dance hostess. When a man came in without a partner they could approach a hostess. They paid 4d a dance and she received a ticket for every dance she had. At the end of the session she got 2d for each ticket she had. In the evenings she taught dancing. The dance hall later became Hazeldines furniture store.

My mother probably met my step father at the dance hall as he was a soldier from Preston Barracks. She married seven years after my father's death and had nine more children. She rarely spoke about my father as it was awkward with my step-father being there, but she did tell my younger sister that she had never met a man like her first husband, he was a real gentleman.

Lottie Scarborough

Opposite: Fred Briggs, front left, father of Lottie Scarborough

18

KEEP THE HOME FIRES BURNING

Keep the home fires burning While your hearts are year-ning
Through the lads are far a-way they dream of home.
There's a sil-ver li-ning through the dark clouds shi-ning
Turn the dark clouds in-side out till the boys come home.

France : Saturday 26 February 1916

Another unpleasant feature about our line - I forgot to mention that three of our men had been killed ... So on the whole it was a pretty nerve-racking time ...

... modern inventions of the Germans have made trench warfare so much more trying: first there are rifle grenades - we have seen enough of the terrible damage they do to have a hearty dislike of them; ... Then there are trench mortars and "minnerverfers", inventions of the devil which descend from a great height and make a most terrifying noise: fortunately you can see them coming and get out of the way if you are lucky. ... Worst of all there is always the possibility of a mine being exploded underneath you ...

However, it is not a pleasant subject, and I have said enough to show you that it is pretty easy to get thoroughly fed up with trench life. ... the snow made the trenches more of a mess than they are already. ...

... it always seems to us so awfully hard to say just the right things, especially when writing home. You don't want to mention nasty things, and yet you must at all costs avoid giving the impression that you are hushing things up. With regard to not grousing, I am often afraid that I have sinned in that direction, ... it does no good and only upsets those at home ... This is not to say that everyone of us does not long for Peace with his whole heart; the utter futility and beastliness of the whole show is constantly brought home to you, and the average man's opinion of war is too lurid for publication. However if I start on this subject I shall never stop, and I might fall foul of the Censor, so I will dry up.

Letter written to his Sister-in-law by George Eric Stevens, born at Preston, Brighton in 1888, died endeavouring to save a wounded comrade in France 13 March 1916 aged 27

My grandfather, who lived at 5 Frederick Gardens Brighton, was one of eight children, four boys and four girls. All four boys served in the army during "The Great War". Grandfather, Richard William Clark Evans joined the Royal Engineers in 1916 at the age of 37. As a married man with four children of his own he need not of joined but as a poster said "Your country needs you".

After training he was sent to France where he remained until early 1919 apart from a few spells on leave in England. Ordinary soldiers only had one or, if very lucky, two trips home a year! Of his three brothers, William Clark, James and Meredith the youngest, two were killed and one lost a leg.

William Clark had joined the royal Sussex Regiment in 1906, he served for several years with the colours then joined the army reserve. He had emigrated to Australia in early 1914, settling in Queensland, but when war was declared he returned to England and re-enlisted 1st November 1914.

He went out to France in January 1915 fighting in several battles there until in 1917 when he was sent to Flanders near Ypres, known as "Wipers" to the men there. On 26th September 1917 he was killed while taking part in the battle for Polygon Wood.

James was also in the Royal Sussex Regiment and was in France. While there he won the Military Medal. Unfortunately he was badly wounded and lost his leg. He died in 1942 but lived longer than his other brothers.

Meredith was the youngest and was in the Royal Army Service Corp. He was sent out to India after being in France, probably attached to an Indian regiment and while there was accidentally killed on 7th May 1919. He is commemorated on a plaque in Madras and has no known grave.

My grandfather eventually died in 1934 in an asylum at Haywards Heath as a result of his experiences during the war, so the effect of the war did not end in 1919 when the armistice was signed; from this family the war extracted a high toll.

John R Morris

I was born on 6th December 1898 in Leyton, London and had five brothers and four sisters. When the First World War broke out I was fifteen years old and working as a paint maker with three friends I had known from school. They were slightly older than me and thought that they would go down to the recruiting office at East Ham, although they were all under age. I had no intention of joining up and the recruiting officer told me to "go home to my mother", but the others said that unless I was recruited they wouldn't join up. I pretended that I was seventeen and eighteen next birthday, which was soon.

On the way to the recruiting office we had seen a soldier with a horse looking very grand; we asked which regiment he belonged to and asked if we could also work with the horses. We were sent to a camp at Crowborough and found that we were in the Horse Transport , looking after the horses not riding them. We then went to Ipswich for six months, then we were put on a ship to Malta. We were sent to relieve the regular army who were sent to the Front, and were called the Voluntary Imperial Service. Malta was the place where the dead and wounded from Gallipoli and Salonika were brought. There were many hospitals on the islands but my job was to keep the horses well groomed and take them to meet the boats and transport the coffins; we used the limbers for carriages for the funerals. I attended hundreds of funerals during this time.

In 1917 we were transported to Marseilles and from there to the Front near Arras. We transported food up to the reserve line of troops - often the horses were killed by shrapnel. We lived in a wagon or a dug-out, sometimes we built a shelter with boards and trees. We had leave every six months. We were paid twelve shillings/- a week and my mother received 3/6d.

When the Armistice was declared I was in Abbeville and a Frenchman dug up three bottles of champagne to celebrate. I visited a prisoner of war camp near Calais and spoke to several Germans. They all seemed decent.

George Morgan

Ethel Chandler and Ethel Chandler with her family

I came to Hove from Holton St Peters, Suffolk in 1912 aged seventeen. The old lady where my aunt was working as cook/housekeeper wanted a house parlour maid, so aunt wrote to mother and asked if I'd like the chance. I thought I'd like to get out and earn a living; father had died and it would help mother if I did. In 1912 my aunt said "Wouldn't it be nice if we could get your mother, sister Hilda and brother Horace down here as well?" She was out walking one day and saw a house for rent at ten shillings a week in Portslade; so when aunt went home to Holton for her summer holidays she helped mother pack up and they moved down here as well

The old lady died just before the outbreak of the First World War, so when war broke out I was working as Cook's Assistant, in a private nurses' home in Portland Road. The start of the war didn't seem to affect us much but it wasn't a very nice feeling when the war broke out, it was awful to think all our men were joining up.

One Sunday in November 1916, my friend the cook from Portland Road and I were talking. I said to her "wouldn't it be nice if we could go into the army?". Funnily enough we were looking down "The News of the World" where they were advertising. We wrote off straight away. We had to go on 2nd December 1916. Mother thought it was dreadful joining the army, she said "I know what I'll send you for Christmas - a packet of cigarettes!" I never did get the cigarettes, I never did smoke but then she knew I wouldn't.

I started in The Women's Legion, where there were Head Waitresses and Waitresses, Head Cooks and Cooks and an Administrator. In July 1917 the name was changed to the WAAC, the Women's Auxiliary Army Corps. When Queen Mary took over as President, it became the Queen Mary Auxiliary Corps. I had all three badges, but I think they are all in a museum in Eastbourne now.

I was at Pirbright for thirteen months, then the Guards wanted their summer camp back, so we had to move to Hazy Down camp, a war-time camp near Winchester. Then of course in 1918 they wanted to get some of them demobbed, so Hazy Down camp was closed and I finished up at Morn Hill. I came home in December 1919.

We cooked for about two hundred army cadets of the Machine Gun Corps, later the Tank Corps, but the numbers dropped as they passed out; we also cooked for the other ranks who had been wounded; they called them detailed men. Reveille went about 6am but we often used to get up before then to be down in the cookhouse by 6 o'clock. We used to have a cup of tea and make tea for the men. We had great big boilers to boil the water up and big tea urns to make the tea in. The men used to do the stoking, keeping the fires going. Breakfast was usually bacon and eggs, or bacon and tomatoes, this was cooked over coal fire ranges, the sort that stood in the middle of the room which you could walk around to keep an eye on the food. Everything was cooked in deep ration tins. We had to start dinner early to get it cooked by 12.30. You had to have the cooked meat ready in the gravy, which was warmed up again in the deep ration tins ready for the waitresses. It was a nice life. You never heard any quarrelling or any distinction among the girls or the men. They were all brothers and sisters, all working together. You knew what you were there for. The Women's Legion was the start of the Women's Army.

Sometimes we used to go to Blackdown Camp, they had social evenings. Or we'd have a whist evening, but most nights I was quite happy to go to my cubicle and go to bed. Some nights you could hear a full military band, as they left to go to the front line. Then you'd hear all the girls crying all night, it was awful to hear, all that crying. I often think of those days.

There was a river which ran by the officers' mess which froze over in the winter and we'd go sliding on it. We had a happy time, but you hadn't to think about what you were there for.

Ethel Chandler

BREWER'S PRAISE FOR WOMEN'S WORK.

Some of the shareholders at the annual meeting of the company on Tuesday found themselves watching through that window a scene such as they could never have imagined possible in any previous year of the long history of the brewery. ...

They were all of them young women, bare headed, with sleeves rolled up above the elbows, the fact that they wore aprons of sacking not concealing the evidence of a splash of colour in blouse or skirt. But these young women one could see from the board room were rolling barrels of beer from one corner of the yard to another; they were carrying boxes filled with bottles; they were bringing up crates and casks for loading on the big steam wagons - and they were doing it with an energy and a determination that left nothing lacking. There was one sturdy young woman lifting up with no apparent exertion casks that many a man passed as "fit for general service" would have hesitated to tackle. The sight was indeed eloquent of the change that has come about in our national life. ...

"If we had not been able to get their labour we could not have carried on the business."

Brighton & Hove Herald 22 July 1916

Women's work in the war, wartime entertainment. With male members of the concert party called up, the show had to go on with three ladies taking the men's parts. A reversal of the Elizabethen situation brought about by the necessity of war

National Baby Week

29th JUNE—5th JULY

EXHIBITION

York Place School,

JULY 1-5

TUESDAY-SATURDAY,

2.30 p.m.-8.30 p.m.

ADMISSION FREE.

Hassall

'Our Children The Hope of the Nation'

Lecture by

DR. MARY SCHARLIEB

AT THE EXHIBITION HALL,

TUESDAY, 3.30 p.m.

Admission FREE.

Prize Babies

At the EXHIBITION HALL,

WEDNESDAY 3=5 p.m.

Admission - SIXPENCE.

For Full Particulars See Handbills.

The Southern Publishing Co., Ltd., 130, North Street, Brighton. K6,921.

My mother, Amy Lee, who later became Amy Jones, was born on 8 June 1892 and lived at 80a Richmond Street, and later at 1 Lower Moulsecoomb Cottages. She left school about 1904 and went into service. She had many jobs including being a cook at Divalls, Smiths in Lewes Road, a greengrocer in Lewes Road and Cooks the Jam Factory.

When war broke out she went to Allen West to work on munitions (picture 1916) and said that while she was there one of the floors collapsed. It was said that the weight of the munitions was too great. Afterwards she was sent to Royal Alfred Sailors Institute at Belevere.

When she returned to Brighton she worked on the trams based at Lewes Road. The photo was probably taken as an advertising feature for a local paper. She had always changed jobs frequently and left the trams when they wouldn't give her a day off when she asked!

Ruby Jones *Opposite: Amy Lee as a tram conductress, and in a munitions factory*

THE WOMEN'S SIDE OF WAR. HELPING THE WIVES AND CHILDREN

Something of what the war means to the women and the children could be seen on Monday in the Brighton Pavilion. There was a pressing throng of women in the outer halls and corridor. These outer halls and the dragon-guarded corridor are no strangers to throngs of "fair women and brave men" women in silks and satins, glittering with gems, who walk to and fro under brilliant lights and amid gay decorations on the arms of gallant cavaliers while "music's voluptuous swell" fills the air with strain of dance measures. But it was a very different crowd of women that thronged the place on Monday.

Here was no gilded and gemmed artifice - only grim, unadorned reality. These were the women who have been left behind by the soldiers called up for the war, as well as by the soldiers who, still in England, are wanted for active home defence. These women made a big, melancholy army. They stood outside under the porch with perambulators; they sat in the entrance halls and on long seats down each side of the corridor; they stood in a packed gathering outside a mysterious door that opened and shut to admit them one by one and was evidently the desired haven of all. Most of them had children with them, girl mothers trying with still unaccustomed hands, so one thought, to still the wailings of infants a few weeks old; sedate matrons holding by the hand children of serious face who were old enough to understand the menace of things, and whose eyes were yet red with weeping farewells. Most of the women were clutching precious papers in envelopes on which one caught the initials "O.H.M.S." One saw, too, marriage lines and birth certificates.

They were there these women, some to receive temporary relief, most of them to prove their right to be registered as recipients of the aid of the beneficent organization which is known as the Brighton and Hove Division of the Soldiers' and Sailors' Families Association. This Association which most of us heard of first during the Boer war is the recognized authority for distributing the nation's relief to the wives and families and dependant fathers and mothers of our soldiers, sailors, reservists, and Territorials. This association, which consists entirely of voluntary workers, giving a considerable portion

MUNITION WORKERS
NOV. 1916

of time to the work, is the channel by which the money subscribed to the Prince of Wales's fund gets into the right hands, so far as the dependants of the fighting forces are concerned.

At first the local Division had to act in an emergency. ... In the first dramatic call for mobilization many families, living at the best from hand to mouth, were left penniless, and during the end of last week there was a rush on the resources of the association from mothers who found that they had no food in the house for hungry little mouths, and no means of getting more. Hungry mouths had to be fed, rules or no rules; and our War Office, which allows grants from its own military funds to mothers, though sure enough, is very slow. So the emergency has been met by temporary grants on the spot to those whose claims passed a quick and not too rigorous scrutiny. Five shillings to each mother and a shilling for each child up to seven shillings in all was allotted, and after some three days of strenuous work, urged on by compassion, the first sharp pinch of distress was tided over. Crowding round the great committee table, which will give room to a full forty, the ladies of the Committee put in a full eight-hour day. By Monday, after a sitting that was not over till well after the average lady's lunch-time, the Committee were able to take breath and feel that the crisis had been tided over.

It should also be noted that the War Office now recognizes not only those wives married on the strength, but also those married "off the strength." This extension of recognition has largely augmented the number of families who will get War Office allowances.

Brighton Herald 22 August 1914

THE WORKHOUSE TRANSFER.

Meanwhile the authorities at the Workhouse are having a very anxious and trying time. The problem of how to remove a thousand people, nearly all of them feeble, and four hundred of them really sick, and to do so without exposing them to suffering, is a serious one. The Clerk to the Board (Mr H. Burfield) and the Master of the Workhouse (Mr Daking) have been working at it day and night. So far they have solved the problem of what to do with the general body of inmates. Some of these decisions involve a curious irony of fate. For instance, the old ladies were removed yesterday to the houses known as "The Lawns," on the sea front out at Aldrington. "The Lawns" were built a few years ago on a scale of luxury and artistic taste rarely equalled in houses with beautiful wood; the fireplaces are curious, the architecture is fanciful; there is every luxury in electricity and warm water. But they seem to have proved too luxurious for ready letting. Now these abodes of artistic luxury are taken possession of by the old ladies of the Workhouse! War brings many whirligigs.

Some of the inmates are lodged at a well-appointed big hotel at Hassocks - much to the scandal of the local Parish Council, who have passed a resolution of horror at this profanation of their stately neighbourhood. Other inmates have gone to Wivelsfield.

The big school that used to be known as Windlesham house, looking down Norfolk-terrace, is also being used.

The difficulty remaining is how to house the sick. The Guardians have fixed upon a houses in Sussex-square and Eastern-terrace as being the only houses suitable for the

purpose. But the owners learning that sick people form the workhouse were to be housed in them. The Guardians have assured them that no infectious cases will be brought, and that no one in the neighbourhood will be able to notice the presence of the patients, but so far the owners have remained obdurate. One hears that, failing a way out, the Guardians will invoke the peremptory intervention of the War Office. But they appeal to the patriotism of the owners, whose objections are seriously delaying the steps necessary to prepare the Workhouse for the reception of the Indian wounded. Surely such an appeal will not fall on deaf ears.

Brighton Herald 5 January 1914

KITCHENER INDIAN HOSPITAL

The Military Authorities officially took over the Poor Law Institution in 1915 and immediately changed its name to the Kitchener Indian Hospital. Their original inspection of the building and its contents revealed some unacceptable equipment. They refused to take over the 177 bedsteads which were of sacking and, according to their Medical Officer, full of bugs. The Institution had only one obsolete steam steriliser and the Operating Theatre they described as "not a very modern one'. The huge ashpit still in use in the grounds was immediately filled in. Despite these deficiencies it was soon to become a vast, fully operational military hospital.

... The hospital originally accommodated 1,500 Indian patients but orders were received to have as large a number of beds as possible. By the middle of June the number was raised to 1,763 and 2,000 by 1 July.

Thirty infectious cases were arranged in groups of five in six wooden huts pallisaded off from the rest of the estate to form an Isolation Hospital. Twenty beds for insane cases were arranged in B Block where four padded cells could be used. Sixty Indian officers were nursed in a separate block and remaining cases were spread among the other buildings."

A History of Brighton General Hospital by Janet Gooch

ARRIVAL OF OUR WOUNDED SOLDIERS FROM THE FRONT ENTERING NEW GRAMMAR SCHOOL BRIGHTON SEPT 1 1914

THE GRAMMAR SCHOOL HOSPITAL

The equipment of the Grammar School in Dyke Road as a military hospital is now pretty well complete. At any rate it is prepared to receive over five hundred patients.

The medical staff consists of eighteen doctors, most of them drawn from the staffs of the various local hospitals, and all with specialist knowledge and experience in medicine and surgery. There are also a further thirteen doctors whose services will be available if they should be required. So far the duties of the medical staff have been confined in the main to examining recruits for various branches of the Army; although they have in addition been called upon to treat a few Territorials who have fallen ill or met with mishap during the process of mobilization and have been removed to the hospital.

The school laundry has been converted into an excellent operating theatre, fitted with an X-ray department and with all the equipment necessary for any operation.

The doctors will be supported by a matron and a full staff of sisters and nurses, many of them from the Sussex County and the other local hospitals.

The administrative staff consists of a Major as Administrator, a Lieutenant as registrar, A Quartermaster, and over a hundred non-commissioned officers and men. The Grammar School has been invested with quite a military aspect. The Red Cross flag floats from the roof, an ambulance wagon stands within the grounds, and men in uniform closely guard the gates.

The Stanford Road Council School has been fitted up as an auxiliary hospital with sixty beds.

The beds have been provided from various sources. there were 100 already in the Grammar School boarding house. A further 80 were sent from Roedean School, and 50 have been loaned by the Brighton Guardians. Others have been given by inhabitants, and a further supply is being purchased from local dealers.

Those of the nurses who have been called up have been billeted at the convent of the

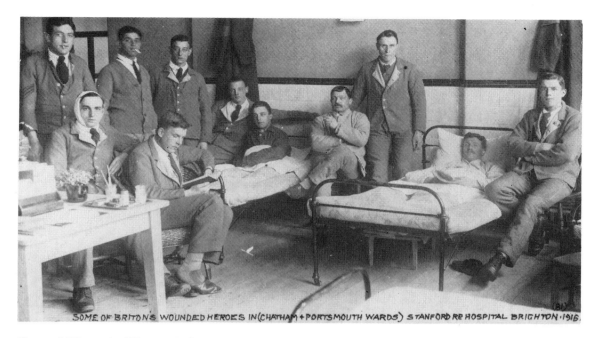

SOME OF BRITON'S WOUNDED HEROES IN (CHATHAM + PORTSMOUTH WARDS) STANFORD RD HOSPITAL BRIGHTON 1916.

Sacred Heart in Upper Drive, Hove. Over a hundred, recruited from various parts of Sussex, are available, although only a part of them have so far been called upon for the work of preparation.

As has been previously explained, the sheets, pillows, and bed clothing for the wounded men have been provided by various working parties acting in association with the headquarters installed at the Pavilion by the Mayoress of Brighton, and by others working in connection with headquarters at the Hove Town Hall.

If need should arise, the Red Cross Society would be prepared with further hospital accommodation at a house at Hove, generously placed at the disposal of the society by Sir Cavendish and Lady Boyle. Here from thirty-five to forty beds could be made up at twelve hours' notice, all the beds and the bedding having been supplied. The nursing would be done by hospital nurses, aided by the members of the Voluntary Aid Detachment, who have all had a certain amount of hospital training.

Brighton Herald no date

A SOLDIER'S FUNERAL CASE FROM BRIGHTON HOSPITAL.

In a peaceful corner of the Brighton Cemetery, far from the boom of cannon and the tearing rush of shrapnel, there lie the remains of a young soldier. He was a victim of the terrible war that is devastating Europe, and is the first to be laid to rest in a Brighton graveyard.

His funeral on Wednesday was accorded all the solemn honours that a military funeral can bestow. There was an armed escort, a body of soldiers to act as coffin bearers, and a firing party to bid a last farewell at the graveside.

The deceased soldier was Private Anton Robert Heren, aged twenty-five years, of the

FUNERAL OF SERGEANT MACKENZIE OCT 14 1914 BRIGHTON.

Duke of Cornwall's Light Infantry. He arrived on Tuesday of last week with the three hundred wounded soldiers who were brought to the Grammar School Hospital. His was one of the few serious cases, for he had contracted rheumatic fever on the battlefield at Mons. Despite skilled attention, Private Heren died on Sunday morning.

A large crowd assembled in Old Shoreham Road to witness the departure of the cortège for the cemetery. They gazed at the line of khaki clad soldiers that was drawn up outside the gates, and at the wounded who sat in the enclosure. It was a strange, moving sight for an English roadside, under a mellow September sun.

Brighton Herald 12 September 1914

In the summer of 1914, the slogan of "Business as Usual" was used to persuade people that society and the economy would carry on much as before, that the war would only be temporary. Detailed plans for the organisation of the war had been drawn up and placed in a "War Book". A Defence of the Realm Act gave the government war-time powers over the individual unknown in peace-time. The navy was mobilised and at sea when war was declared. A small regular army, superbly trained and equipped for another Boer war, was swiftly mobilised and shipped across to France, where it was expected to play a minor role on the left flank of the much larger French Army; short term measures aimed to fight a war without disturbing British society greatly. But the British people soon found that the war was not to be over in a few months; the German attack had smashed straight into the British Expeditionary Force, the French Army also suffered terrible losses.

The enthusiasm of the volunteers survived the poor conditions, lack of equipment and the rigid discipline of an army that could not respond to the intelligence and energy of these new recruits.

Even before the carnage of the Somme, the British Government reluctantly realised that the war could not be continued on the volunteer system. The supply of volunteers for the front was drying up, casualties were too heavy and manpower had to be managed to maintain both the army and the home front to support it; so a third army of conscripts came into being. The introduction of conscription in 1916 was a decisive moment in British history, before its introduction, despite recruiting campaigns and pressures on individuals amounting almost to blackmail, it had been an individual's choice to fight for his country. With this compulsion came a change in attitude to the war. A small number had conscientious objections to fighting, but most of their grounds were rejected, and they were treated harshly by the government and public opinion. Many more went on the run, or evaded the dangers of front-line service. Among those "who obeyed the call" there was less enthusiasm, yet morale did not break.

Front line soldiers lived in terrible conditions and with the fear of almost inevitable death or mutilation. The average life expectancy of a junior officer in the front line was six weeks; a man who entered the infantry in 1916 was lucky if he survived until 1918. Some men were wounded once, sent back, wounded again, and finally killed when they returned to the front for the third time. Men hoped for "Blighty wounds", injuries severe enough to get them out of the trenches and home honourably, without damaging their bodies permanently.

Combined with this fear was the cold, squalor, boredom and fatigue of trench existence, the horror of seeing a friend killed or terribly wounded, the harsh discipline and meaningless routine imposed from higher up. But loyalty to friends, the fear of showing fear, severe military discipline, and perhaps a grim patriotic determination to see the thing through, and not be beaten kept these men in the trenches.

Although the horrors of war were almost completely confined to the armies in the trenches, loss and bereavement were experienced by nearly every family. Letters from the front were censored, and most soldiers tried to hide the full horror of war from their loved ones, but the scale of death was obvious in the casualty lists, the obituary columns and crowded military hospitals. The telegraph boy became a messenger of death, bringing official notification and regrets from the War Office, that a father, husband or son was dead, wounded or missing.

Before the war, many sections of the working class had suffered chronic unemployment, low wages and low status. As more men left for the army and the demands of the war economy increased, unemployment came down and wages went up. Many soldiers, existing on a private's pay felt bitter envy at the high wages earned by men employed in "war work".

The position of women changed dramatically. Women had worked before the war, but their jobs were usually badly paid and of low status; for the duration of the war, women were recruited into areas of work which had been closed to them, especially after the introduction of conscription.

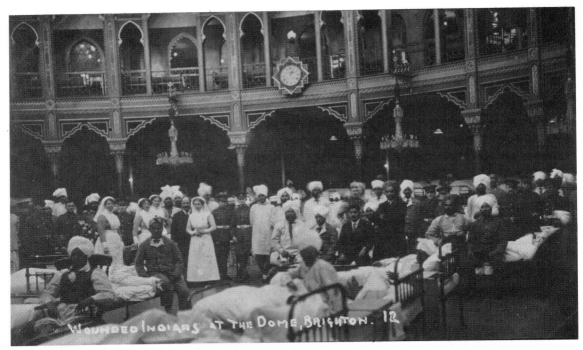

Wounded Indians at the Dome, Brighton. 12

The Royal Pavilion Hospital

When Britain declared war on Germany in 1914 there were only some 7,000 hospital beds available in the United Kingdom, insufficient for nursing the casualties expected from the Western Front. Many Poor Law institutions were taken over for use as military hospitals and the Brighton Workhouse (now Brighton General Hospital) was rapidly transformed into the Kitchener Hospital. More unexpectedly, when the jewel in Brighton's crown, the Royal Pavilion, was offered by the Corporation to the King, this too was designated by him as a military hospital, specifically for Indian soldiers wounded in France. He felt, it is said, that they would appreciate the Indian surroundings, although in fact the interior of the Pavilion reflected Chinese rather than Indian styles of decoration. There are stories of men, recovering consciousness amid these unexpected splendours, who believed that they had awoken in paradise.

The first Indian expeditionary force (there were to be three others, sent to different theatres of war) began landing at Marseilles in September 1914, and eventually numbered 70,000 in France. Some five and a half thousand of these would be killed, and well over sixteen thousand wounded. On arrival the men were rapidly moved up to the Front, and immediately deployed in the generally water-logged trenches, hastily dug across the British sector, which was defending part of northern France and Flanders. The incessant rain and bitter cold of an early winter resulted in many cases of frostbite, trench foot and gangrene, to add to the many more injuries resulting from machine gun fire and high explosive. By November 1914 the Indians had already suffered over 1800 casualties.

The Indian wounded evacuated to England were nursed in special military hospitals, mainly in Brockenhurst and Brighton. The Pavilion, together with the Dome and Corn

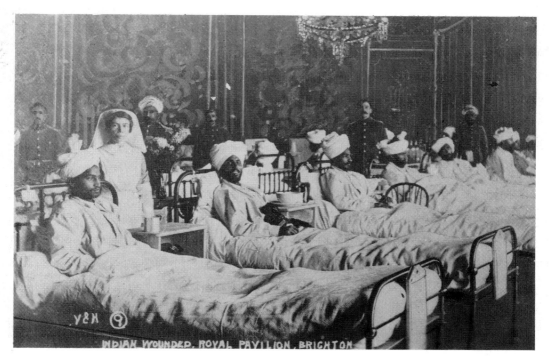
INDIAN WOUNDED, ROYAL PAVILION, BRIGHTON

Exchange, provided 724 beds, and the Kitchener, initially intended for 1,500 Indian patients, later could accommodate 2,000. A third Indian hospital was established in York Place.

Very careful preparations were made to ensure that the ritual requirements of the different religions, practised by the various communities among the Indian soldiers, could be met. The largest single group within the Indian Army was composed of Sikhs, who were mainly from the Punjab. The Gurkhas from Nepal, and the Dogras and Garhwalis from neighbouring areas in the Western Himalayas were all Hindus, as were the Jats who came, like the Sikhs, from the Punjab. There were also Punjabi Mohammedans, as well as Mohammedans from Madras and the Deccan, while the Pathans and the Afridis from the North West Frontier region and the neighbouring Baluchis were also adherents of the Muslim faith. Separate arrangements were made for the different caste, religious and linguistic groups. The Sikhs at the Pavilion worshipped in their Gurdwara on the lawns, and the Mohammedans prayed, five times a day, as enjoined by their religion, and facing Mecca, on the grass plot in front of the Dome. All notices were printed in Urdu, Hindi and Gurmukhi. Two water taps were provided in each ward, one for Hindus and the other for Muslims.

At the Pavilion there were nine kitchens, generally located in huts on the lawns, providing separate cooking and washing up facilities for the Muslims, for meat eating Hindus and for vegetarians. Special arrangements had to be made for the ritual killing and storing of the meat.

There were separate bathing houses and latrines, and separate mortuaries. Hindus and Sikhs who died were cremated on the Downs near Patcham, on the site now occupied by the Chattri, an Indian memorial to the dead; their ashes were scattered on the sea. In fact

35

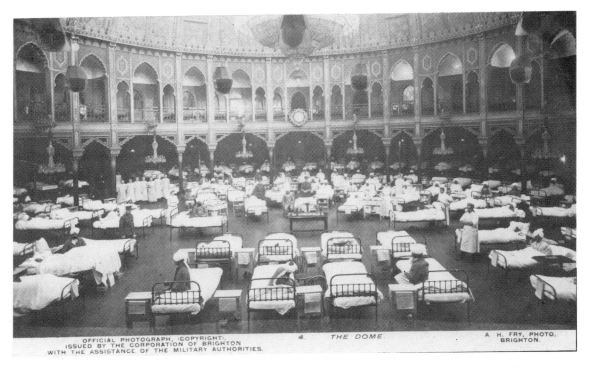

4.   THE DOME

there were only 32 deaths in the Pavilion hospital, but it has to be remembered that many of the more seriously wounded did not survive the agonising journey to England.

Medical and surgical treatment was the responsibility of British doctors and surgeons of the Indian Medical Service or the Civil Medical Service in India, all of whom would have been proficient in at least one of the Indian languages. The sub-assistant surgeons were drawn from the Anglo-Indian community, while the writers and clerks were Indian. It was claimed that there were no female nursing staff at the Kitchener hospital, as these were thought to be out of place in an Indian unit, but contemporary photographs show that British nurses, were caring for the wounded men at the Pavilion, as their colleagues were doing at the base hospitals and on the hospital trains in France. Ward orderlies were appointed of the appropriate caste; and there were untouchables - separately housed - to carry out the duties of sweepers and dhobis.

The majority of cases treated were gunshot wounds, and these required to be x-rayed, explored under anaesthetic and drained. Dressings were often pads of sphagnum moss enclosed in muslin. At the Pavilion there were operating theatres in the Prince Regent's kitchen and the Church Street entrance to the Dome. Near the main entrance to the Pavilion were facilities for radiant heat treatment and for 'galvanisation, ionisation and fadadization" and for giving local applications of electricity. The Drawing Rooms, Saloon, Music Room and banqueting Room were all wards and the smaller rooms served as isolation rooms or offices. At the Kitchener Hospital there were special quarters for those patients diagnosed as insane.

The decision at the end of 1915 to withdraw the Indian Army corps from France for re-assignment to Mesopotamia and other theatres of war meant that the Indian hospitals in Brighton were vacated in January 1916, to be used for the remainder of the war for nursing British and Dominion casualties. The curiosity of the townspeople with regard to the exotic patients who had previously been nursed at the Pavilion was at last satisfied, when during the first week of February it was open to the public. By February 9th there had been over 10,000 visitors. Many of those who paid their 2/6, 1s or 6d must have recalled the excitement in the town when distinguished soldiers (among them Lord Kitchener), statesmen and politicians had visited the Indians, and above all the honour accorded to them by the King-Emperor himself when on August 25th 1915 he had held an investiture on the Pavilion lawns. Among those decorated was Subadar Mir Dast VC. His tribute to the Pavilion Hospital, reported by the Times of India in January 1916 was simply, ... "I received the kindest of treatment."

Joyce Collins

The war hospitals in Brighton were part of a massive medical effort required to deal with the terrible human wreckage of war. In 1914 the Royal Army Medical Corps consisted of two hundred doctors, nine thousand medical orderlies and five hundred and sixteen nurses; by 1918 there were 10,700 doctors, 115,000 orderlies and 6,000 nurses. Romantic fantasies of quick and heroic deaths in battle, or simple wounds in mentionable places, were soon overtaken by reality. Most of the wounded were mutilated by high explosive shells or their health ruined by gas. In 1929, 2,414,000 men were in receipt of a war disability pension, they ranged from 1,907 suffering from flat feet caused by the war, to 40,000 partially blinded, and 65,000 in hospitals from shell-shock.

In some respects the wounded during the 1914-1918 war had advantages over men wounded in earlier wars. Antiseptics meant many more survived surgery and anaesthetics meant that surgery could be more drastic; but X-ray investigation and blood transfusion were in their infancy and much trauma surgery was developed as a result of World War experiences. For most soldiers wounded in the front line, the journey back to a base hospital was long, agonising and dangerous. Sometimes they were left stranded in no-man's land for days before they could be safely brought back in. Stretcher parties of eight men would spend long hours manhandling the wounded men through mud, over shell holes and enemy fire. The battle field was filthy and there were ever-present dangers of wounds being infected by gas-gangrene or tetanus. Many wounded died on the way back to the Regimental First Aid Post, where the lucky survivors could be given first aid and passed back to hospitals in the rear. Even in the base hospitals treatment was primitive and painful. Most wounds turned septic, there were no antibiotics to treat them.

AWARDED THE MILITARY CROSS.

LT. VERE BENETT-STANFORD, R.F.A.

For conspicuous gallantry during operations. During a fortnight he did fine work as liaison officer with the infantry, and as F.O.O. He shewed the greatest courage and resource under heavy shell-fire. At great personal risk he went out to the assistance of an officer who had been seriously wounded, and also of a wounded man.

The Stanfords & the Gobles

The Stanford family

In 1914 the Stanfords of Preston Manor could be considered the first family of Brighton. Charles Thomas had married into the Stanford family and became Charles Thomas-Stanford. Ellen Stanford was Lady of the Manor. Charles Thomas Stanford was a Justice of the Peace and one of the Conservative MPs for Brighton. He had been Mayor of Brighton between 1911 and 1914. He was to remain in Parliament until 1922, receive the freedom of the town in 1925 and become a Baronet in 1929. Ellen Stanford was the direct descendent of the first William Stanford (1764-1851). Vere, the young First World War artillery officer, was her grandson. There was a great rift between Ellen Stanford and her son John Montague, who outlived his son Vere, dying in 1947; but there was a great bond between Ellen Stanford and her grandson, Vere. Had he not died in 1922 it is probable that Vere would have continued the Stanford line at Preston Manor.

The Stanfords were a typical upper class Edwardian family. Charles Thomas-Stanford had been to Oxford reading law, before going off to South Africa to become a friend of Cecil Rhodes and make money in diamonds. Initially a Liberal, he became a Conservative-Unionist, because he was against Home Rule for Ireland and a believer in Britain's Imperial Destiny. Ellen played the Edwardian lady's role supporting her husband and a number of "Good Causes". Vere, her grandson, had the traditional education of his class, preparing him to become an officer and a gentleman. He went from a prep-boarding school to his father's old house at Eton, then on to the college for artillery officers at Woolwich. He was commissioned into the Royal Field Artillery before the start of the war.

The material on which this short account of the family during the war is based comes mainly from the scrap-books kept by Ellen Stanford between 1914 and 1918. These books contain letters and documents which illustrate the stresses and strains of the long war on a family which had a wide circle of friends and family all involved in the war. They also show the many duties undertaken by a "prominent member of the community" in the war effort.

There is no doubt about the commitment of the Stanfords to "a just war" against an evil enemy. Charles becomes a staunch supporter of the Lloyd-George coalition government and chairs recruiting rallys in Brighton. He supports the introduction of conscription and speaks against conscientious objectors in the House of Commons. Ellen Stanford is worried about possible German spies in Brighton and writes to the Chief Constable about this matter. However, she mainly concerns herself with the traditional duties of welfare and charity undertaken by the Lady of the Manor. She dispatches cigarettes to the "Tommies", games and comforts to the "Jolly Jack Tars", while also concerning herself with the poverty and hardship of the women and children left behind. Toys are distributed to the children of men serving at the front, food and clothing are collected and distributed to the needy, and committees formed to oversee this charitable work. Very much the activities of a "Lady Bountiful" in peace time, but on a much larger scale. The suffering has to be dealt with but is not questioned.

But anxiety and bereavement were also experienced more closely. She sent many letters of comfort and condolence to friends who lost sons and husbands in the war. The scrap books contain replies to her letters along with a newspaper obituary for the man concerned. These items are a personal insight into the sorrow and tragedies of the war. They also show how deeply engrained religious and patriotic beliefs were among these respectable middle-class families. Perhaps the idea that these sacrifices had been made in vain would have been unbearable.

However Ellen Stanford was more concerned with the welfare and safety of four particular men who went to war and who appear frequently in the scrap books. Remarkably they all survived, although her grandson, Vere, died soon afterwards from the effects of gas on a fragile constitution.

"Croppy" *(opposite)* was the family nickname for Harry Vere Benett, an interesting member of the Stanford circle. He was the illegitimate son of Ellen Stanford's first husband, Vere Fane Benett, but this was no bar to his friendship with the Stanford family, nor did it hinder a successful career in the army. He wrote many letters to the Stanfords throughout the war, about the happy times he had had at Preston Manor, how much his thoughts return there, how much he appreciates their letters and his concern about how the family are coping with the war. He became a lieutenant-colonel and undertook mysterious missions for the War Office. As a linguist and Russian speaker he joined the military mission in St Petersburg and gave vivid accounts of the Russian revolution in 1917. He remained in Russia and played a part in the British military intervention against the Bolsheviks in 1918 and 1919.

The second man, Oswald Mansell-Moulin, was not a member of the family, but a contemporary and close friend of Vere Benett, Ellen Stanford's grandson. He became a pilot in the Royal Flying Corps, was shot down and there was great anxiety as to his fate. The Stanfords were able to use their influence and through the American ambassador in Britain were able to discover that the young man was safe in a prisoner-of-war camp long before any official notification came through. Ellen Stanford's interest in him continued and broadened into a more general concern over the living conditions of British prisoners-of-war and civilians interned in Germany.

A nephew, George Eric Thomas, starts the war as a midshipman on one of the Royal Navy patrol vessels in the Channel and writes frequently to his aunt and uncle at Preston Manor, describing life on board a small ship, thanking them for their gifts and proudly announcing his promotion to sub-lieutenant. He reproves his uncle for using his political influence in attempts to get extra leave for him.

The last of the four men was Vere, grandson, heir and tragedy of the family. He was commissioned into the Royal Field Artillery as a career officer before the war started. He served throughout the war as a front line officer and at one time, aged 23, was reputed to be the youngest major in the British army. He wrote many letters home and does not hide the dangers and discomforts of trench warfare; he shows a robust ruthlessness in enjoying the shelling and killing of Germans. He was twice wounded, once slightly, but his wounds were more severe on the second occasion and he was out of the war for a year with both physical and psychological damage. On one occasion he gave his gas mask to a sergeant and receives a dose of gas that weakens his lungs, so that after the war he succumbed to tuberculosis. Although there are signs of physical frailty before the war, he accepts the horror of the trenches as a patriotic necessity, and seems typical of the young men of his class who went off to fight the war.

The final tragedy of his death and the extinction of the Stanford line does not occur until some years after the war. At the armistice the Stanford family seems intact and successful. Charles Thomas Stanford, as a supporter of Lloyd George, is re-elected as MP in the Khaki Election of 1919. He presides over several victory celebrations in the hope that pre-war conditions would return; but they did not. Eventually, Preston Manor became the property of Brighton Borough Council.

OBITUARIES AND LETTERS IN PRESTON MANOR.

L. C. P. Roberts, missing 14 August 1916.

Distressing anxiety has fallen to Mr. H. D. Roberts, the Director of the Brighton Library, Museum and Art Gallery by the tidings that his brother, Lance-Corporal Percy Roberts has been missing since the middle of July. Prior to the war L. C. Roberts was at the head office of the Union of London and Smith's Bank. He joined up immediately after the outbreak of war.

Extract of a letter to Mrs Stanford from H.D. Roberts

I am sorry to say that we have no further news of my brother. I have had several letters from other men in the 10th Royal Fusiliers, but all of a negative nature. He has now been missing since July 15th and by a coincidence this evening's post brings the official intimation that he is missing. We are dreadfully upset as he was our youngest and favourite brother. One would think that if he had been wounded and picked up by another regiment we should have heard by now. ...

Obituary: Captain Gerald Charles Stewart, adjutant of the 10th Royal Hussars, who was killed in action in Flanders on May 13th, was born in 1888. He was educated at St. David's Reigate, Harrow and Sandhurst, and was gazetted to the 10th Hussars in Feb. 1907. He was appointed adjutant and promoted Captain in 1912. He was twice wounded in October. He was the eldest son of Mr. Charles John and Lady Mary Stewart.

Extract of a letter to Mrs Stanford from Charles Stewart:

Very many thanks - I know that you feel for us - one has the great comfort that our boy like the other brave fellows who have fallen have done their best in perhaps the greatest issue ever fought for. When one puts self out of consideration one could not wish it otherwise.

Obituary: Langley - On the 31st October 1917 of wounds received in action the previous day, Trooper Robert Frank Langley, New Zealand Mounted Rifles transferred D.A.C. New Zealand Field Artillery, elder son of Mr. and Mrs. A. E. Langley, Kawiha, New Zealand, and nephew of Professor Langley, Cambridge. Aged 24.

Extract of letter from Professor Langley, Nov. 25, 1917, to Ellen Stanford

Dear Mrs. Thomas -Stanford

It is very kind of you to write. My nephew was a fine, strong, vigorous youth who made friends wherever he went. We were deeply attached to him. He survived Gallipoli but was mortally wounded in passing through a barrage in France. His only brother has also been killed at the Front. In this and in thousands of other such cases it is the women who suffer most - mothers who never recover from the loss, daughters and sisters left without the intimate friendship and support they have looked to. In face of the desolation of innumerable homes I do not understand the frame of mind of those who are ready to renew relations with Germans after the war ...

The Goble family

Before the Fourteen Eighteen War we lived in Upper Lewes Road. My mother and father ran a coal merchants business in Islingword Road, but my father had died when I was very young and the family were renting rooms in Southover Street in 1914. I had two older sisters and a brother.

Albert Goble aged 18 in the centre : Edwin & Albert, 'Bert' Goble (seated) on leave

I was an apprentice with the Brighton & Hove General Gas Company but I thought that I would go to the recruiting office and join up. The recruiting office was at the Royal Pavilion and the officer gave me a shilling to go and get a copy of my birth certificate. I wasn't quite 18, but they still accepted me, I was sent to Chichester and then to Suffolk, to join the mounted brigade. I thought "mounted" meant we would be with horses, but we were all issued with bicycles. I was an officer's servant in Suffolk. We did coast patrol at night.

The Suffolks were sent to France and landed at Calais. I immediately managed to catch trench fever and spent three weeks in a field hospital at Etaples. I asked for permission to go up to the line to rejoin my regiment. Unfortunately I never caught them up and I was placed with the London 60th Rifle Brigade and stayed with them until I was discharged. I was in France for twelve months and caught trench fever again, when I was in Belgium. This time I was in the field hospital and all the other patients were German. I celebrated my twenty first birthday in that ward and Matron made me a cake. I think she liked me, because she asked me to go and work for her after the war, but I said that I had my own plans.

I was used as a runner between the lines and the base. We spent one week in the trenches with no change of clothes and very little to eat and then we would be relieved and go back to camp to wash, rest and be fed. Once we were playing marbles in the trenches and a friend jumped up and was shot straight through the head, it was awful.

When I eventually returned to Brighton my family no longer lived there. My brother Edwin had been in the Dragoon Guards Band, which didn't leave England, and he had settled in London. My two sisters Dorothy and Grace both went to work in London; the youngest did war work in the Houses of Parliament basement, the eldest had some sort of shop work; my mother had eventually gone to London to be with them. I had assumed that I would get my job back with the Gas Company but they said that as I had volunteered to go into the Army I would have to go to the back of the line. I decided to retrain and moved to London to join the Civil Service.

Albert Goble

I was born Margery Goble, a first cousin of Albert Goble, at 57 Richmond Street, Brighton where I lived with my older sister and parents. We attended Finsbury Road school. I was five when war broke out.

My father was 39 or 40 and was not called up, but he volunteered in 1916. He worked for a firm of estate agents called Dewdney and Collins at the top of St James's Street and his boss volunteered so I think he felt he should as well. As he was older he was not sent overseas but joined the Royal Flying Corps as a member of the ground staff and went to the North of England. We didn't have the same worry as those with fathers overseas, but there were bombs where he was, and some of his friends were killed.

Money was short when my father joined up as my mother received £1 for herself 5/- for my sister and 3/6d for me and the rent was 9/- a week (I think 2/- was paid for additional children). Food was short and there was rationing of certain goods. It was rather haphazard and you snatched what you could, when you could, meat, sugar, butter and margarine were short and mother would send us down to the shops as soon as she knew that a consignment was in. We lived near the town so we were near Liptons, Pearkes and Home and Colonial.

I remember feeling hungry on occasions, but it wasn't because there wasn't good food around. Most people kept a few chickens and so there were fresh eggs and a lot of people had allotments so there was fresh vegetables. Money was short and so mother took in visitors from London who came to escape from the 'Taubes' bombs and Zeppelins. My sister and I slept in my parents' bed and Mother slept in a single bed in the room. This left two rooms that she could let and we had visitors from London, who stayed for several weeks. I think they brought their ration books with them, and bought the food for mother to cook. We knitted socks for the troops and mittens for the milk ladies who took over the delivery of milk when the men left. Women also worked on the trams and at Allen West on munitions and many did nursing.

I lost two cousins in the war, one was shot by a friend while cleaning his rifle in 1915. He hadn't realised it was loaded and it went off accidentally and shot him through the heart. The man was devastated and visited my aunt after the funeral and always kept in touch with her. My cousin, Leo Howell was blown up right at the end of the war.

On the 11th November the maroons went off, horses stopped, men got off bicycles and trams and buses stopped. Men took their caps off, even in the rain, and stood absolutely dead still. You could hear the leaves dropping off the trees and children would fight hard not to cough.

The Armistice was in 1918 but peace didn't really come until 1919. It was then that the troops came home. Thousands and thousands were killed, everyone hated the Kaiser and you could not like the Germans. The sense of hatred went on for a long time.

There was a lot of unemployment after the war and they marched along the seafront singing to make people notice them. People were very poor for some time until the 30s.

Margery Botting

1 Frank Goble, shot by a friend's gun. 2 Percy Goble, brother of Frank, wounded but survived; his son, Frank was killed at Arnhem in the Second World War. 3 Alfred Goble, father of Margory Botting in his Flying Corps uniform

UNVEILING OF BRIGHTON
WAR MEMORIAL
BY EARL BEATTY OCT-7-1922

D-M-W (9)
BRIGHTON

End of the War and Aftermath

The war started at the beginning of the second week of the Sussex Fortnight when the holiday season was in full swing. The Brighton and Hove Gazette announced, "Brighton has resolved to keep smiling." On the 22nd of August the paper reported that Brussels had been captured by the Germans and also that Brighton is itself again." It was hoped that Brighton would attract new fashionable visitors who would be unable to journey abroad in 1915. The shelling of East Coast resorts by German warships made people shift their holidays to the South Coast, and Zeppelin raids on London meant that Brighton was a safe haven. There were fewer day trippers, but Brighton became a fashionable resort for those trying to forget the rigours of war. It had "escaped the terrors existing only a few miles away and its comparative peace and security were the secret of the remarkable influx of people." (Brighton & Hove Gazette)

But there were others whose situation in Brighton was not so rosy. The town had always had a large community of foreigners, many Germans and Austrians who were employed in the hotel and catering trades suddenly found themselves to be "enemy aliens", liable to arrest or deportation; their place was taken by French and Belgian refugees. The service industry was disrupted by the outbreak of war causing unemployment; above all the families of men who decided to volunteer who suddenly found themselves without a breadwinner.

Throughout the war Brighton remained disunited in sorrow. "The town was filled with members of the royal families and the aristocracy of Britain and Europe, the wives of wealthy industrialists and financiers, with actors, actresses and popular journalists; fashionable Sunday morning parades on the sea front continued. ... The Brighton Gazette reported, "the tripper element was eliminated" and their commentator confessed, he was 'almost inclined to ask "Is there a war on?" ' In fact the name of Brighton became somewhat of a by-word in the popular press as a resort especially frequented by "profiteers", munition millionaires and other vulgar "nouveau riche" who rubbed shoulders with the aristocracy in the grand hotels of the town." (Life in Brighton by Clifford Musgrave)

But life in wartime Brighton was not so rosy for most Brightonians; 2,597 men and three women of Brighton are listed on the war memorial as having died for the country in the First World War. In the last winter of the war hardship amongst the Brighton poor led to a well organised demonstration which declared "The wives and children of our fighters shall not want for food." After the war ended Harry Cowley organised a "Vigilante" movement to move homeless people into squats in empty property. If 1916 was bad, 1917 was worse and in the early summer of 1918 the Germans broke through the British lines. In the early years people had asked "When will the war end?" and optimists answered "In a few months or next year." In the latter stages the questions put were "Will this slaughter ever end?" "Can it be ended?" The propaganda machine talked of ultimate victory but many people hoped at best for a stalemate.

Living standards fell as the war machine made even greater demands on the economy, and the German U Boat campaign strangled the sea lanes. Rationing was introduced in February 1918, as scarcity had made it inevitable. Wages rose, but so did prices. In the late summer and autumn of 1918, quite suddenly, the Germans were defeated. They were even more starved and exhausted than their opponents, and the arrival of the Americans tipped the balance against them. The November Armistice was greeted with joy and relief, but it was overtaken by the great influenza epidemic which killed more civilians (150,000) in the winter of 1918 than had died throughout the war.

In the aftermath of the war there was a great gap between the ideal and reality. The ideal was symbolised by the war memorials put up all over Britain, in every city, town and village. On the 11th hour of the 11th day of the 11th month of each year there would be two minutes silence and powerful ceremonies to remember the war dead, not cynical ceremonies and symbols foisted on the British by their rulers, they were accepted by a people that needed to come to terms with the Great War, a token of a promise "that they had not died in vain", jobs and "homes fit for heroes" for the returning survivors.

Reality was to be different; there was a Ministry of Reconstruction in 1918, and plans for advances in education and housing, but by 1922 most of these plans were in ruins. A short term post-war boom soon collapsed, followed by long years of inter-war unemployment. It was once again "Business as usual" and "Back to 1914".

Meanwhile ordinary people had to pick up the pieces: war widows, war spinsters and blighted lives; single parent families created by war, with the mother struggling to bring up children on an inadequate war pension. Families having to support a father or son unable to work, because many men came back blinded, lacking limbs, disfigured or ruined psychologically for the rest of their lives. Even the lucky ones came back suffering from "nerves". The war did not only change the lives of individuals, it changed attitudes and behaviour.

I was born in Surrey but my family moved to Brighton when I was eleven, and we lived at 3 Coombe Terrace. I had five sisters and five brothers. My baby sister is now 87. I left school aged twelve, and went into domestic service.

In 1914 I was living with my husband and two children in St Martin's Street. My husband had been born in this house as had our children. He was a blacksmith's strike at Brighton station and he was called up to fight in German East Africa. He returned in 1918 with a tropical disease and died in 1919. I did not get a pension to start with because he did not die in the war; I had to go out and do housework to support my children. I didn't have help from anyone, there was no British Legion or anything like that.

It was my son's school teacher who helped me get a pension. He belonged to the Soldiers and Sailors Association, and he helped me make my claim for a pension. I had to go to London and be interviewed. They had lost my husband's papers and his will, but at the end of it I got a small pension. God came with me that day.

Kate Harmer

I had a sweetheart at home who I'd known at school called Lillie. Her mother became very frightened of the bombing in London and moved to Brighton. I married Lillie while I was on leave in Brighton in January 1918. I lost contact with my three friends, Harry Hawes, Tommy Bessborough and Fatty Butler. As I didn't return to Leyton I never knew if they survived.

I returned to Brighton and couldn't get a job. There was a queue up the road from the Labour Exchange, hundreds of us, but there was no violence. As I had worked with paint I was told that there might be a job at Eversheds at Portslade. There wasn't a job, but when the owner found out that I had walked there he gave me a ten shilling note.

Eventually I found work and lived in Brighton with my family.

George Morgan

The war that people said would be over by Christmas entered it s fourth year and by the end of the summer there were hopes of a settlement, then on November 11th 1918 an Armistice was signed in a railway coach.

November 11th 1918 was a dull foggy day and in the evening our Father took us down to St Peter's Church to hear the bells being rung for the first time since the war started. Life began to get back to normal again. There were more potatoes and sugar, and people were pleased to eat real white bread again.

Hilda Barber

The flu epidemic reached Brighton in 1918. A lot of people contracted it and died. My mother and I both caught it and my aunt came to look after us. She stayed two or three weeks and we recovered, as a result of good nursing.

Some of the schools closed to stop the infection spreading. At Finsbury Road School the teachers used to come round with a puffer with pink powder in it to get rid of the germs.

As there was no radio or television the newspaper was the only means of communication, but children did not read the papers, so I was unaware of how serious the flu epidemic was. Children were more likely to die in those days and rarely went to the doctor, as it cost too much. We were used to seeing funerals, so I don't suppose I thought it was unusual seeing so many at this time.

Margery Botting

A mysterious and disastrous epidemic that killed more people throughout the world than the Great War itself. The Spanish Flu, a septic influenza suddenly began its ravages in the spring of 1918, further upsurges occurred in the winter of 1918 - 1919. In little over a year it killed twenty million people world wide, perhaps sixteen million of them in India. Its onslaught in Europe caused 166,000 deaths in France, 225,000 in Germany and nearly 229,000 in Britain. The figure for Britain is astounding when you compare it with 1,500 civilian and 750,000 military war dead in the previous four years.

Contrary to perceived opinion the disease did not kill many of the old or those weakened by war-time deprivation; most of its victims were the young. In cemeteries on Salisbury plain lie scores of young New Zealand and Australian soldiers, too late for the Western Front, but not for the flu epidemic. Something like three quarters of the population were struck down. Lloyd George himself was put to bed in

Manchester Town Hall for ten days shortly after the Armistice. Cinemas and theatres were closed, a state of affairs not achieved by the war, and people only ventured into public places with gauze masks covering their mouths and noses.

The flu epidemic demoralised a people already shattered by war, then disappeared as rapidly as it had come.

Deaths Exceed Births

As one of the consequences of the war, the deaths in Brighton & Hove last year outnumbered the births. In Brighton the deaths exceeded the births by 43 and in Hove by 119.

In Brighton the percentage of illegitimate children was 12.21, as compared with an average of 7.6 for the four years preceding the outbreak of war. This shows that the number of illegitimate children came somewhat near last year to being doubled. As the total number was 229, it is probably safe to class 100 of them in the ranks of the much discussed "war babies".

Brighton & Hove Herald 5 October 1918

Sisters United in Death

In truly pathetic circumstances the grave has been closed this week over the remains of two sisters Miss Mabel Guildford and Miss Alice Guildford. It will be recalled that we chronicled last week that Miss Mabel Guildford had passed away at her home in Brighton after an illness of only five days from pneumonia, following upon influenza. During her illness she had been nursed by her sister Alice with that devotion that had characterized the two sisters throughout their life. In her turn Miss Alice Guildford was seized with the malady, and as the remains of her sister were being borne from the house for the funeral on Tuesday, she herself breathed her last. The double affliction that has thus fallen upon the widowed mother is nothing short of tragic, and sympathy has flowed out to her in heartfelt sincerity. That sympathy has been extended to the brother, Lieutenant C.J. Guildford, who some six weeks ago had been invalided home from France to a London Hospital with trench fever. Summoned to Mabel's deathbed, he was able to get to Brighton just before she died.

Brighton & Hove Herald 26 October 1918

THE WAR-BLINDED MEN OF ST. DUNSTAN'S. BOOT-MAKING.—IN THE LECTURE ROOM (NOTE BLIND AND NEARLY DEAF MAN "LISTENING IN").

The St Dunstan's Institute for people blinded on war service was founded in 1915 by Sir Arthur Pearson. By 1918 nearly 2,000 men blinded during the war were rehabilitated. The first convalescent home in Brighton opened in 1918 at West House in what is now 12-14 Portland Place. The purpose built building at Ovingdean Gap, Ian Fraser House, was opened in 1937.

The Shoreham Mutiny

SHOREHAM & SOUTHWICK MEN MARCH TO BRIGHTON

Mayor and Chief Constable Interviewed; MAYOR'S GOOD ADVICE

The most remarkable military demonstration ever witnessed in Sussex took place this morning, when 7,000 from the London Command Depot at Shoreham and the Royal Marine Engineering Works at Southwick marched to the Brighton Town Hall to protest against the delay in the demobilization of the troops.

Every man of the 7,000 has served overseas, and for some time past, it appears, they have been labouring under a sense of injustice at the inequality of the treatment they allege has been meted out to them. Throughout yesterday the leaders of the men were busy enlisting promises of the support of the troops to march out of Camp today, and at 7 o'clock this morning they took active steps towards carrying out their object. The General-in-Command, having been appraised of the men's intentions, addressed them from the flagstaff on the question of demobilization. He pointed out that thousands of troops could not be demobilized without some delay, and promised that if they had a genuine grievance he would forward it to the proper authorities. He offered to meet them again at 11 o'clock, but the leaders of the men decided at once to march into Brighton, and shortly afterwards the whole route from the camp was alive with masses of khaki-clad men. At Southwick they were joined by men of the RME, and on the way to Brighton every soldier in the streets was invited to join in the procession.

The Brighton Town Hall was reached shortly after 11 o'clock, and steps were at once taken to secure an interview with the Mayor through the offices of the Chief Constable. ... Meanwhile the troops formed up in Bartholomews, and, in thoroughly orderly fashion, whiled away the time in songs and a few speeches. ...

"We demand demobilization as soon as possible," said this man, who was wearing two wound stripes. "There is far too much messing about," he proceeded, "doing physical jerks, washing up pans and dishes, and generally doing women's work while we might be at home doing our own jobs. Why cannot we be discharged in khaki if they like and sent home, and if they want us they know where to find us. If we were home we could go and find a job, but we cannot do it while we are confined to Camp.

Evening Argus 6 January 1919

THREAT OF STRIKE AT SHOREHAM

Further demobilization demonstrations took place today, in London, Bristol and Shoreham. The weather kept the men in camp at Shoreham, but had the morning been fine Worthing was to have been visited like Brighton was yesterday. ...

A general demobilization, despite all the demands, cannot be ordered until the Peace Conference because it is necessary that Mr Lloyd George, and those who attend the Conference from this country, should know that they have an army behind them. An efficient organization must be maintained to enable Great Britain to meet any contingency during the peace negotiations. ...

The following is a copy of a telegram sent to the Prime Minister from the disaffected soldiers at Shoreham Camp:-

We men of the London Command Depot, the 1st Siege Artillery Reserve Brigade and the Training Wing situated at Shoreham-by-Sea, Sussex, bring to your notice the following resolution:-

That we demand the instant demobilization of all men here by being sent home pending demobilization papers being forwarded to us, thereby enabling us without delay to return to civil life.

The inclement weather conditions had interfered with a projected march to Worthing, and this assembly took place instead, the great enclosure being packed to the doors, and a great number being unable to gain admittance. Without any demure the men decided to stand by their original resolution, which was to the effect that every man, irrespective of whether he has work to go to or not, should be returned to his home to await demobilization papers going through, instead of being kept in uncomfortable surroundings and doing absolutely nothing.

The meeting was addressed by a general officer who informed them that their grievances had been handed to Sir William Robertson, who was at the present moment in conference with Lord Milner. the meeting had also been advised that the London Command Depot was prepared to demobilize 25 men in each company per day; but it was unanimously decided by a vote to stand by the original resolution. The outcome was the telegram to the Prime Minister already mentioned.

Everything is quiet and orderly at the camp.

A further meeting of the men at Shoreham Camp this afternoon, it transpired that it had been arranged to demobilize 250 men per day at the London Command Depot. The case of the RGA men has not yet been settled. It was decided that the London Command Depot men should resume their military duties until satisfaction had been obtained for them.

Between the two meetings to-day a prisoner, who it was declared was being victimised, was released by a party of the men.

Evening Argus 7 January 1919

R.G.A MEN RESUME DUTY Spirit of Patriotism: Shoreham

A meeting of disaffected RGA men stationed at Shoreham, who have abstained from duty during the past two or three days mainly on account of the slowness of demobilization, took place at camp this morning. The message from Mr Lloyd George, which has appeared in the Press was read out to the troops, who were also addressed by their commanding officer and the men, in a spirit of patriotism, decided to carry on with their duties, and to trust to those in authority to remedy their grievances as quickly as possible.

Evening Argus 9 January 1919

The best organized, if not the largest, show of disobedience took place at Shoreham, Sussex. The thousands of soldiers gathered in that camp, all of whom had seen service overseas, organised themselves, elected a committee, and decided on a strike.

The reason for their grievances was that they considered the methods of demobilization were most unfair. Men who had been in the Army only a few weeks or months were being demobilized because their bosses could pull a few strings in the right quarter whilst others who had been right through the war from the beginning were still patiently waiting....

When the mutiny broke out the officers tried to crush the uprising by the usual Army methods of putting the mutineers in the guard room on a charge. A mass raid on the guard room would then take place and all the prisoners released. This occurred on many occasions...

Just as long as the arrests continued, so long did the men refuse to parade or to carry out their orders; but when the commanding officer gave up the attempt, some men did co-operate in cleaning and in other duties. "There was no interference from the others when they did so. No punch ups or anything of that description. Problems of administration were decided by a committee elected by the men, but the commanding officer remained in nominal control: "On the whole it was an orderly affair." ...

Why did the army give way at Shoreham and discharge so many men so quickly? There are no official reasons given, but a number of considerations must have carried weight. In the first place, up to seven thousand troops were out on strike and showing exceptional determination: "short of putting them up against the wall and shooting the lot", it was hard to see how discipline could have been restored. Second, neither time nor place were suited to a show of force. This was no wartime camp in France, but Brighton two months after the Armistice. Third, it was doubtful whether the army had sufficient loyal troops in England to put the demonstrations down.

The Unknown Army: Mutinies in the British Army in World War One by G Dallas & Douglas Gill

The British Army was the only European Army engaged in the First World War that did not undergo a mutiny or mass surrender. There were cases of "Loyal Indiscipline" and riot, notably at the base camp at Etaples in 1917 when men protested against harsh discipline, but no British troops refused to fight. At the end of the war there was unrest in the army over the slow pace of demobilisation. there was distribution amongst troops in London, Hastings, Dover and Calais, but the biggest army demonstration broke out at Shoreham and culminated with the march to Brighton. The British Government looking at the Bolshevik Revolution in Russia and similar events in Germany and Hungary were fearful of social unrest in the country. There had been a number of bitter shocks in the summer of 1915, including a strike of 12,000 London Police for recognition of their union. In Ireland, a guerrilla war that was developing into a full scale military campaign, was to end in partition in 1921. Perhaps the government exaggerated the possible revolution in this country and gave in to the demands made by the soldiers of Shoreham.

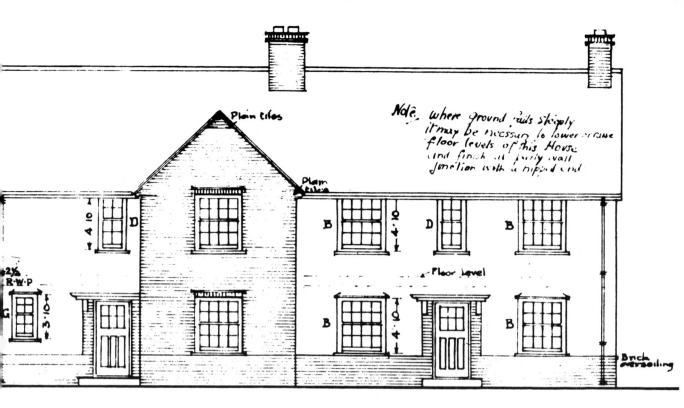

Note, where ground falls steeply it may be necessary to lower or raise floor levels of this House and finish at party wall junction with a hipped end

Plain tiles

Plain tiles

Floor Level

Brick oversailing

Homes for Heroes

• FRONT ELEVATION •

Moulsecoomb

Brighton is to have a model garden suburb - but not, of course, until after the war. Definite progress, however, is being made with the scheme to build 1,000 houses near Brighton, and it is possible that something more may be heard of the project at the next meeting of the Town Council. The proposal, as far as can be gathered at present, is to build about ten houses to the acre. It is the intention of the Corporation to engage the highest expert advice they can get in order to ensure that the estate on which the houses are to be built shall be laid out on the most attractive lines. There is to be no dead uniformity of what might be called "modern prettiness' about the modern garden suburb. All the houses are to be of an individual character. All are to be fitted with electric light and baths and are to have a reasonable amount of garden. What is most important of all, they are to be let at a rent which make them self-supporting. But at the prices to which building materials are soaring- and no one anticipates that house prices will fall for many years to come- it does not seem clear how the rent can be a moderate one.

Brighton & Hove Herald 29 June 1918

"One of the earliest, and one of the best Council housing estates in England", writes Antony Dale in The History and Architecture of Brighton.

The Bishop of Chichester wrote in 1939 in the preface to a pamphlet Rents in Moulsecoomb, "Everybody who goes along the Lewes Road must admire the appearance

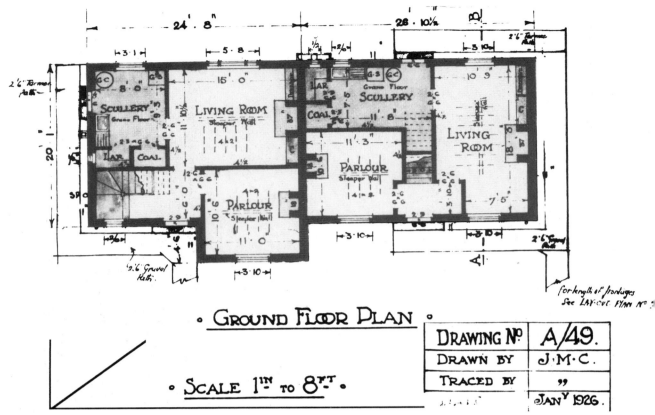

GROUND FLOOR PLAN

SCALE 1ᴵᴺ TO 8ꜰᵀ.

DRAWING Nº	A/49.
DRAWN BY	J.M.C.
TRACED BY	,,
	Janʸ 1926.

of the three Moulsecoomb housing estates; the layout and the style of building. Externally they do credit to Brighton Corporation and to the architects, surveyors and builders who brought it into being." In the same pamphlet Marion Fitzgerald wrote of the "Pleasing aspect and sound construction of the houses."

There was at this time [1920s] an enormous amount of commercial building development especially at Patcham, Ovingdean, Woodingdean and Rottingdean, but the standard of design and layout of these houses was in general far below that of the municipally planned estates. In some areas of private speculative development not one house appeared to have been designed by an architect. On the other hand, the Corporation's housing estates at North and South Moulsecoomb were among the most imaginatively laid out housing schemes in the country, ranking almost equal with the famous garden cities of Letchworth and Welwyn.

Peacehaven

Whilst the war popularised the romantic ideal of rural England, it also encouraged the association of land with freedom; it was, after all, what people had been told they were fighting for ... the move out to plotlands following the war reflects the idealisation of the rural with a strong strain of agrarianism thrown in. Many men who had been told they were fighting and dying for an England which was at its very best in the countryside, naturally wanted something better on their return from the war than the life many of them had left behind in the urban slums. For years before the war, political parties had been promoting the idea that life in the countryside was 'naturally' healthier for the people, and therefore for the nation, and suggesting various means of encouraging people to 'return' to the land. The end of the war, and the failure of Governments' 'Homes for Heroes' campaign was the impetus for many of those who could afford it to buy a stake in the land they had been fighting for. It is not surprising that many of them rejected the controlled tenancy of small holdings, and chose instead to purchase a stake in the land which was most accessible to them; the plotland developments.

...two main strands [run] through the ... promotion of Peacehaven: the health giving properties of life on the South Downs, and the freedom which ownership of a plot of land gave to the plotholder. ... the healthiness of life on the Downs was a major selling point ..., and life in Peacehaven was often compared favourably to life in the towns; a cartoon published in 1921 showed "types of people not found in healthy Peacehaven", whilst a comparison with the nearest large town stated that in "Brighton, they are always saying good health, up here we are always having it."(Peacehaven Post October 1921).

With so many men returning from the war with impaired health, the 'health-giving breezes' of life upon the Downs probably held a large appeal, and many disabled ex-servicemen decided to invest their service pension in a new life in Peacehaven. A Mr Sayers,who had been gassed in the war, bought three plots of land after being advised to leave London by his doctor. According to the Peacehaven Post, Peacehaven was just the place for ex-servicemen like Mr Sayers to invest their pension, and reported walks around the estate almost always included a 'chance' meeting with recuperating residents, such as "Mr Sanderson, visibly rejuvenating", and his neighbour Mr White, disabled in the war and advised to move to a healthy spot. (Peacehaven Post October 1921). A healthy country life had an increased attraction for those injured and disabled by the war; life in Peacehaven was an accessible means of achieving this. ...

The many people who moved to Peacehaven in the 1920s were, in a way unforeseen at the time, fulfilling the hopes of those who had been concerned about the future health of the English race. However, Peacehaven was as much a legacy of the idea of 'land for the people' as it was a legacy of the ideal of a peaceful, stable rural Arcadia. For many of its inhabitants, life in Peacehaven held the promise of freedom.

The [Peacehaven] Post argued that life in Peacehaven was a free life; a life free from the cares and stresses of city life, free from the fears about health, and free from worries about finding the rent. Ownership of land gave the plotholders the freedom to grow some of their own food. Admittedly, this could also be achieved through tenancy, or carefully monitored ownership of smallholdings, but life in Peacehaven was free from almost every form of land control: "a little plot of freehold Mother Earth at Peacehaven is a thing of safety and joy forever." (Peacehaven Post September 1921).

In the first years of peace, the talk was of 'reconstruction', and building a new society. A move 'back to the land' seemed a pleasant way of starting afresh, abandoning the bad old ways of the towns whilst recapturing the best of 'Old England' which the war had supposedly been fought for. The [Peacehaven]Post was quick to link Peacehaven with this rebirth of England, explaining that: "When this country, worn and war-weary, woke one morning to find the guns had ceased and the smoke had cleared away ... it was then that the word 'Peacehaven' breathed its way into many a home in many a town. (Peacehaven Post November 1922).

Peacehaven was to be the ideal home of the new England: egalitarian, peaceful, young and free, a co-operative community ... where men who have done their bit will find a tranquil, healthy, sunny home for their retirement. (Peacehaven Post October 1924).

However, this very egalitarianism of Peacehaven could be a drawback as well as selling point. Many of the plotholders could afford to buy plots of land but could not afford to build on them ... this resulted in many of the plots remaining vacant, eventually leaving the development with a scattered, haphazard appearance. Many plotholders who could afford to build could do so only with the cheapest materials, creating a landscape of caravans, wooden shacks and half-finished bungalows, interspaced with the grander villas which wealthier plotholders had been able to build. This shanty-town appearance was further enhanced by Neville's policy of selling plots without services, which left the town with one made-up road and the distressing lack of a sewerage system. All this was a very far cry from the 'Garden City by the Sea' which Neville had intended to build, and which he continued to advertise Peacehaven as.

... Although Peacehaven had begun as a sort of 'brave new world', in a time of reconstruction and brave speeches predicting: " ... not perhaps the Golden Age, but an age which is brightening form decade to decade, ... from which we can see the things for which the heart of mankind is longing," (Woodrow Wilson 1918), it ended the 1920s apologetically, trying to fit itself into the southern rural Arcadia which it was seen to have invaded. As the 1920s progressed, they had seen the end of the post war idealism and hope; the slump, rising unemployment and the relative failure of the Governments' 'Homes For Heroes' campaign had all contributed to making pre-war England seem an innocent, idyllic time of peace and prosperity; the last days of a lost 'Golden Age'. Although to its inhabitants Peacehaven may have seemed the rural idyll they had been searching for, to its attackers it was one of the worst developments of the modern age, encroaching on a part of rural England which was central to ideas of Englishness, and symbolising the lack of social control and breakdown of order which seemed to typify the post-war age.

In a competition to choose a name for the new estate, "New Anzac-on-Sea" was chosen as the winner; but as a result of representations that Anzac was almost a sacred word, following the tragic events of Gallipoli, it was not a name which could suitably be used to advertise a new seaside place, so this was later changed to Peacehaven. In the original plan, dated 1916, for Anzac-on-Sea many of the streets were named after first World War battles: Louvain, Marne, Mons, Loos, Festubert, Salonica and Ypres Avenues. These were later changed to: Gladys, Sunview, Vernon, Southdown, Seaview and Friars Avenues. It was obviously not possible to sell plots of land on avenues bearing names which reminded people of the tragedies of these First World War battles.

About this book

This book was made by: Michael Corum, who wrote the introductions and about the Stanford family; Lucy Noakes, who wrote about Peacehaven; Joyce Collins who wrote about the Royal Pavilion as a hospital; Martin Evans; Eleanor Beatty; Hazel Marchant; Irene Donald; John Roles; David Beevers; Alistair Thomson; Marion Devoy; Elfrida Oldfield, Aelie Munro, Jacqueline and K R Connatty; Selma and Dicon Montford; and Christine Park without whose help this book would not have been possible.

Tony McKendrick-Warden, Brighton Museum, Preston Manor, Brighton Reference Library, Jacqueline Connatty and several authors have made photographs available from their collections. Brighton Borough Council's Plan Registry provided plans of a house in North Moulsecoomb. Bob Seago of Media Services at Brighton Polytechnic prepared photographs, documents and posters for publication.

Cover: Peter Messer of Art and Design.

Published by the Lewis Cohen Urban Studies Centre at Brighton Polytechnic, 68 Grand Parade, Brighton BN2 2JY tel: 673416 or 643113 and QueenSpark Books, 68 Grand Parade, Brighton.

December 1991

Printed by Delta Press, South Wing, Level 1, New England House, New England Street, Brighton BN1 4GH.

Copyright © the Lewis Cohen Urban Studies Centre at Brighton Polytechnic and QueenSpark Books.

ISBN No: 0-904733-55-6

The Lewis Cohen Urban Studies Centre at Brighton Polytechnic

The Lewis Cohen Urban Studies Centre at Brighton Polytechnic is an information and resource centre concerned with understanding the local environment.

Book List : if ordering by post please add 50p per book to cover postage and packing, cheques payable to Brighton Polytechnic

Whose Welfare: Private care or public services? Peter Beresford & Suzy Croft (1986) £8.95

A History of Hollingdean (1986) £2.00

Housing and Women in Brighton and Hove by Rachel Lickiss (1987) £3.00

Resources for Environmental Education (1988) £3.00

The Provision of Information to Council Tenants by Rachel Lickiss (1988) £3.00

Providing Information About Public Services by Rachel Lickiss (1988) £3.00

The Windmills & Millers of Brighton by H T Dawes (1989) £3.00

Backyard Brighton: photographs and memories of the thirties (with QueenSpark Books 1988 & 1991) £4.95

Backstreet Brighton: photographs and memories of the fifties and sixties, a sequel to Backyard Brighton. (with QueenSpark Books 1989) £3.95

Out & About: places to visit around Brighton, Hove & Lewes by Rachel Lickiss (1989) £3.00

Brighton Behind the Front: photographs and reminiscences of life in Brighton during the Second World War. (with QueenSpark Books 1990) £3.95

Blighty Brighton: photographs and reminiscences of life in Brighton during the First World War. (with QueenSpark Books 1991) £4.95

Streetwise: a quarterly magazine published for the National Association for Urban Studies, subscription rates on request.